Brain & Mind

Psychology

Dr. Hasan Yahya

مطابع القدس

ISBN-13: 978-1477634202
ISBN-10: 1477634207
Mental Voyage Series - 6

Manufactured in the United States of America

Author and Subject

Internet communication in rapid modern times makes readers look for short and concise articles and Novels. This book is a voyage for two minutes with the writer to enjoy this mental trip into medical science.

The author is an Arab American scholar, writer & professor of sociology. Dr. Yahya has four children and ten grandchildren and live in Lansing Michigan, USA.....

From (P.8)

Here is an example, may bring more understanding of the difference between the brain and the mind, "The brain is the engine, while the car is the physical body of the human being where the mind is the driver of this car of life."

Introduction

This book includes articles on Brain and Mind applied to three categories: learning, wisdom, and awareness. These articles on science of brain and mind and the relations between both and the three variables.

Mind refers to the aspects of intellect and consciousness manifested as combinations of thought, perception, memory, emotion, will and imagination, including all of the brain's conscious and unconscious cognitive processes. In the first part the relationship between the brain and mind is explained. An enduring mysteries of science equal in importance to the quest for a unifying theory connects general relativity and quantum mechanic.

The second article shows the extremely important matter that we know exactly which - the brain and/or mind is in charge of one's own perception using our ability as a tool to use awareness.

The third article, describes the relation between mind and wisdom. Just as "Wisdom" is defined by its attributes. Subjectively, mind manifests itself as a stream of consciousness..

As the mind runs the show of living, behaving and acting out life within the parameters of the script provided by the brain, the fourth article, describes the relation between mind and learning. When the mind/self is heavily trapped under the cloak of the brain it generates patterns the full mind/self/I/me is still there, and people can become awakened to their true self. It is a very slow process but once we start on the self awareness journey each step makes it easier for the next step. Awakening our true self and strengthening the self, even listening to our true self we can and will save us from all this brain pattern inflicted hurts and pain and restlessness not as a part of our life. All these emotional holes that we tolerate and think that they are a part of our human nature. Awareness makes it possible to completely align the brain mind relationship where the brain and mind both perceive actual-reality as actual-reality.

Brain and Mind

A series of articles written in the process of Arab Manifesto Philosophy sponsored by the Arab American Encyclopedia-USA

1

The relationship between the mind and the brain is one of the enduring mysteries of science, equal in importance to the quest for a grand unifying theory between general relativity and quantum mechanics.

The brain defined, a physical body that develops into a super body when the exercise it gets is provided by super mature parents. When the exercises provided are by premature, immature and mature parents then the brain develops physically into a projector that projects a premature, immature or mature mind/self.

The mind runs the show of living, behaving and acting out life within the parameters of the script provided by the brain. The brains script writing abilities are restricted by the amount of emotional intelligence that the brain is powered by. Each progressive stage of the brain is actualized as the earlier emotional intelligence is replaced by a more mature emotional intelligence. The brain is the projector that runs on the power provided by the developed emotional intelligence potential.

Here is an example, may bring more understanding of the difference between the brain and the mind, "The brain is the engine, while the car is the physical body of the human being where the mind is the driver of this car of life."

The mind drives the show of living, behaving and acting out life within the parameters of the script provided by the brain. The brain however, is the engine, while the car is the physical body of the human being where the mind is the driver of this car of life.

In other words, the brain is like the small child, the teenager, the adult and or the master. The mind is the manager. The manager has access to reality while the child, the teenager and to some extent the adult lives in his own dream world. First and foremost they both have overlapping hardware. Where the brain develops this hardware that the mind totally depends on. So the quality of the brain supplied hardware on which the mind depends determines the minds own quality. However the silver lining in all this is the true self is also very much real and this true self also supplies the mind with its own input. The true self often shows its frustration in the form of our so called conscience. So when one is feeling guilty then the mind and the true self are feeling guilty. Of course sometimes the mind feels guilty while the conscience is neutral and vice-versa. As when one applies for a job and is turned down because of lack of skills; then the mind knows that the self has screwed up by not developing the skills needed to get the job. But the true self is frustrated as it is the self image that has screwed up.

In conclusion, many theories were found in the literatue, to explain the relationship between what we call your mind (defined as the conscious thinking 'you' which experiences your thoughts) and your brain. In fact, it's fair to say that this is one of the fields of philosophy which is most up in the air (although, of course, all of philosophy is up in the air to some greater or lesser extent). www.askdryahya.com

The human mind is consciousness that manifests itself as the self and the self is the mind that manifests itself as consciousness.

It is not hard to observe how the connection between the brain, mind, self image, consciousness, self and conscience! And even the connection between the mind and wisdom. I also see a clearer picture of the Id, Ego and Super Ego according to Frued. The description of mind, in some textbooks is mentality according to The World of Psychology by Samuel E. Wood and Ellen R. Green Wood.)

There we go again. Just as "Wisdom" is defined by its attributes, the mind is also defined by its attributes! So the mind also is mentioned by its attributes! Wikipedia has the following definition: Mind (pronounced /☐ma☐nd/) refers to the aspects of intellect and consciousness manifested as combinations of thought, perception, memory, emotion, will and imagination, including all of the brain's conscious and unconscious cognitive processes. "Mind" is often used to refer especially to the thought processes of reason. Subjectively, mind manifests itself as a stream of consciousness....

According to the Webster dictionary the mind is:

1 : recollection, memory (keep that in mind) and (time out of mind)

2 : the element or complex of elements in an individual that feels, perceives, thinks, wills, and especially reasons or the conscious mental events and capabilities in an organism c : the organized conscious and unconscious adaptive mental activity of an organism.

So we are speculating that the self image is the mind which manifests itself as consciousness; consciousness manifests itself as the mind. Or better still consciousness is the mind that manifests itself as the self and the human mind is consciousness that manifests itself as the self. The self image is the face of the mind. The mind is the self conscious self image. Unfortunately for most of us consciousness gets stalled at a lower level and so for all practical purposes our consciousness is the mind's own image that manifests itself as the self image.

Conscience, however, is the highest form of consciousness and is the highest humanness potential which means it is the real you. The pure you is your conscience. Your conscience is the Christian, Muhammad and the Buddha or any imagined sacred person in you.

The mind runs the show of living, behaving and acting out life within the parameters of the script provided by the brain. It is extremely important that we know exactly which - the brain and/or mind is in charge of one's own perception and the tool for this is our ability to use awareness.

Awareness is when one's true self, one's mind, the 'I', free of the entrenched brain patterns is able to reflect on the full context of the brain mind relationship and its resultant out comings - how we perceive our own mind/self/'I'/'me', how we perceive others and how we perceive the full context of our life. Awareness is in play when we identify our self with the mind and focus our mind/self/'I' on what we perceive our self to be. When we observe our self from the point of view of Mother Nature/actual reality. When we observe not only the context of our current life and why it is the way 'I'/we are; we also review our options of what the mind/me/I/self can be. With our mind's eye, the other name of awareness, we must understand the consequences/context of our brain controlled self.

Human behaving and acting out of life within the parameters of the script provided by the brain, the brain decides how extensive the potential horizon of the mind will be. Life's potential is provided by the brain's developed emotional intelligence. This emotional intelligence is the power that defines the power of the mind/self.

Even when the mind/self is heavily trapped under the cloak of the brain generated patterns the full mind/self/I/me is still there, and once you become awakened to your true self, you can gradually chip away at the entrenched brain patterns which are buried in the unconscious. It is a very slow process but once you start on the self awareness journey each step makes it easier for the next step though sometimes it may even be necessary to take out side help.

Awakening our true self and strengthening the self, even listening to our true self (which often flares up as our conscience) we can and will save us from all this brain pattern inflicted hurts. All this stumbling through life, all these hurts and pain and restlessness need not be a part of our life, even group and country's life. All these emotional holes that we tolerate and think that they a part of our human nature we can fill/remove through awareness. Awareness makes it possible to completely align the brain mind relationship where the brain and mind both perceive actual-reality as actual-reality.

These brain patterns are caused by the buried hurtful memories that keep playing like broken records. In our unconscious we still keep blaming our self for all the hurts, pains, insults, fears etc. So we take out these buried memories in full awareness of our current actual reality. We re experience the actual past pain, fear just the way we felt when it happened. While at the same time focused on the current reality.

Awareness helps us to put our whole life in context. It makes us aware of our own personal reality especially as it relates to our actual reality. It gives us a 'third party' awareness, an awareness of an outside observer observing one's own self/mind. Not only do we become knowledgeable about our 'outside in' perception patterns and our 'inside out' perception patterns it even gives us the discrepancy between the two. It is this discrepancy that creates all the problems from poverty to restlessness to hunger for more and more and every thing in between.

The goal of awareness is to bring our personal reality (P-R) in line with the real world - the actual reality(A-R). Awareness shows us the gap between the two. In fact the internet is an example full of ways how to fill this gap - by enabling the brain mind relationship to become physically and emotionally super healthy. www.askdryahya.com

Brain, Mind & Learning

2

The mind runs the show of living, behaving and acting out life within the parameters of the script provided by the brain.

It is extremely important that we know exactly which - the brain and/or mind is in charge of one's own perception and the tool for this is our ability to use awareness.

Awareness is when one's true self, one's mind, the 'I', free of the entrenched brain patterns is able to reflect on the full context of the brain mind relationship and its resultant out comings - how we perceive our own mind/self/'I'/'me', how we perceive others and how we perceive the full context of our life. Awareness is in play when we identify our self with the mind and focus our mind/self/'I' on what we perceive our self to be. When we observe our self from the point of view of Mother Nature/actual reality. When we observe not only the context of our current life and why it is the way 'I'/we are; we also review our options of what the mind/me/I/self can be. With our mind's eye, the other name of awareness, we must understand the consequences/context of our brain controlled self.

The mind runs the show of living, behaving and acting out of life within the parameters of the script provided by the brain. It is the brain that decides how extensive the potential horizon of the mind will be. Life's potential is provided by the brain's developed emotional intelligence. This emotional intelligence is the power that defines the power of the mind/self.

Even when the mind/self is heavily trapped under the cloak of the brain generated patterns the full mind/self/I/me is still there, and once you become awakened to your true self, you can gradually chip away at the entrenched brain patterns which are buried in the unconscious. It is a very slow process but once you start on the self awareness journey each step makes it easier for the next step though sometimes it may even be necessary to take out side help.

Awakening our true self and strengthening the self, even listening to our true self (which often flares up as our conscience) we can and will save us from all this brain pattern inflicted hurts. All this stumbling through life, all these hurts and pain and restlessness need not be a part of our life, even group and country's life. All these emotional holes that we tolerate and think that they a part of our human nature we can fill/remove through awareness. Awareness makes it possible to completely align the brain mind relationship where the brain and mind both perceive actual-reality as actual-reality.

These brain patterns are caused by the buried hurtful memories that keep playing like broken records. In our unconscious we still keep blaming our self for all the hurts, pains, insults, fears etc. So we take out these buried memories in full awareness of our current actual reality. We re-experience the actual past pain, fear just the way we felt when it happened. While at the same time focused on the current reality.

Awareness helps us to put our whole life in context. It makes us aware of our own personal reality especially as it relates to our actual reality. It gives us a 'third party' awareness, an awareness of an outside observer observing one's own self/mind. Not only do we become knowledgeable about our 'outside in' perception patterns and our 'inside out' perception patterns it even gives us the discrepancy between the two. It is this discrepancy that creates all the problems from poverty to restlessness to hunger for more and more and every thing in between.

The goal of awareness is to bring our personal reality (P-R) in line with the real world - the actual reality(A-R). Awareness shows us the gap between the two. In fact the internet is an example full of ways how to fill this gap - by enabling the brain mind relationship to become physically and emotionally super healthy.

There are two emotional powers, one for the brain, the other for the mind. While the brain reacts, the mind reflects and then acts. The management and control is the domain of the mind. The initial feedback is that of the mind. The five senses are a mixed domain. The current environment is absorbed by the mind. Which passes the information to the brain. The brain references this information with its stored patterned emotional reactions from the past and tries to interpret the new information as the same old information. And tries to act as if nothing has changed, while life is always about change.

Emotional holes are the domain of the brain. The worry about having emotional holes is the domain of the mind.

In education the education of intelligence that is of say math and science is geared in a way that both the mind and brain work on the same page. In the case of emotional intelligence the emotional intelligence is frozen in the brain while the mind tries to absorb the current information as that is what it knows. When the new information of the mind is different from the assumed as same past information of the brain there is a conflict. Which ever is more powerful dominates.

Instead of hearing as if just one voice is coming from a single source; you got to train your self to hear the voice of the brain, mind and your true self as it comes from them individually. Then you have to focus your third eye - your focused mind on the voice of the brain and put the causes of this voice in contextual mindfulness. You gradually take the steps to ultimately blend the voice of the brain, mind and the true self into one single voice. It will be the voice of the mind that will ultimately be your true voice as your mind having developed to its full potential will be also the voice of your true self.

The main factor of emotional intelligence is what the brain understands the self to be. The brain produces the emotional intelligence and the mind runs on this emotional intelligence. It is like the mind is employed by the brain or the brain is employed by the mind. The brain pays the mind in emotional intelligence power(EIP/emotional mind power/EMP). The mind/self/I then spends this EMP with little degree of independence at the premature mind level. With a mixed freedom at the immature level and with much freedom at the mature level. And with full freedom at the super mature level.

The EMP of even the lower level when awakens and made aware of its dominance by the emotional brain power(EBP) can be focused to measure its own outside in reality. It can be made aware of how much of its full EMP is developed, how much is stalled and how it can be fully developed.

Understand how EBP is reflected in life: it is reflected in the degree of self importance. At the premature emotional brain power level it is reflected in an omnipotent self image. At the immature emotional brain power level it is reflected in a corrupt self image. At the mature emotional brain power level it is reflected in a trophy self image. At the super mature emotional brain power level it is reflected by a an image less selfless self. At the super mature level the EBP and the EMP blend into one heck of a brain/mind power behemoth.

The brain understands and the mind knows. The trick is to change the understanding of the brain where ever the understanding is below par. The real self in all this is always there chained to the brain level. The potential to become super mature for the true self is blocked by the EBG in the brain. As the EBG is removed the self potential is actualized.

Brain, Mind & Wisdom

3

The human mind is consciousness that manifests itself as the self and the self is the mind that manifests itself as consciousness.

It is not hard to observe how the connection between the brain, mind, self image, consciousness, self and conscience! And even the connection between the mind and wisdom. I also see a clearer picture of the Id, Ego and Super Ego according to Frued. The description of mind, in some textbooks is mentality according to The World of Psychology by Samuel E. Wood and Ellen R. Green Wood.)

There we go again. Just as "Wisdom" is defined by its attributes, the mind is also defined by its attributes! So the mind also is mentioned by its attributes! Wikipedia has the following definition: Mind (pronounced /☐ma☐nd/) refers to the aspects of intellect and consciousness manifested as combinations of thought, perception, memory, emotion, will and imagination, including all of the brain's conscious and unconscious cognitive processes. "Mind" is often used to refer especially to the thought processes of reason. Subjectively, mind manifests itself as a stream of consciousness....

According to the Webster dictionary the mind is:

1 : recollection, memory (keep that in mind) and (time out of mind)

2 : the element or complex of elements in an individual that feels, perceives, thinks, wills, and especially reasons or the conscious mental events and capabilities in an

organism c : the organized conscious and unconscious adaptive mental activity of an organism.

So we are speculating that the self image is the mind which manifests itself as consciousness; consciousness manifests itself as the mind. Or better still consciousness is the mind that manifests itself as the self and the human mind is consciousness that manifests itself as the self. The self image is the face of the mind. The mind is the self conscious self image. Unfortunately for most of us consciousness gets stalled at a lower level and so for all practical purposes our consciousness is the mind's own image that manifests itself as the self image.

Conscience, however, is the highest form of consciousness and is the highest humanness potential which means it is the real you. The pure you is your conscience. Your conscience is the Christm Muhammad and the Buddha or any imagined sacred person in you. . www.askdryahya.com

Brain, Mind & Awareness

4

The mind runs the show of living, behaving and acting out life within the parameters of the script provided by the brain.

It is extremely important that we know exactly which - the brain and/or mind is in charge of one's own perception and the tool for this is our ability to use awareness.

Awareness is when one's true self, one's mind, the 'I', free of the entrenched brain patterns is able to reflect on the full context of the brain mind relationship and its resultant out comings - how we perceive our own mind/self/'I'/'me', how we perceive others and how we perceive the full context of our life. Awareness is in play when we identify our self with the mind and focus our mind/self/'I' on what we perceive our self to be. When we observe our self from the point of view of Mother Nature/actual reality. When we observe not only the context of our current life and why it is the way 'I'/we are; we also review our options of what the mind/me/I/self can be. With our mind's eye, the other name of awareness, we must understand the consequences/context of our brain controlled self.

The mind runs the show of living, behaving and acting out of life within the parameters of the script provided by the brain. It is the brain that decides how extensive the potential horizon of the mind will be. Life's potential is provided by the brain's developed emotional intelligence. This emotional intelligence is the power that defines the power of the mind/self.

Even when the mind/self is heavily trapped under the cloak of the brain generated patterns the full mind/self/I/me is still there, and once you become awakened to your true self, you can gradually chip away at the entrenched brain patterns which are buried in the unconscious. It is a very slow process but once you start on the self awareness journey each step makes it easier for the next step though sometimes it may even be necessary to take out side help.

Awakening our true self and strengthening the self, even listening to our true self (which often flares up as our conscience) we can and will save us from all this brain pattern inflicted hurts. All this stumbling through life, all these hurts and pain and restlessness need not be a part of our life, even group and country's life. All these emotional holes that we tolerate and think that they a part of our human nature we can fill/remove through awareness. Awareness makes it possible to completely align the brain mind relationship where the brain and mind both perceive actual-reality as actual-reality.

These brain patterns are caused by the buried hurtful memories that keep playing like broken records. In our unconscious we still keep blaming our self for all the hurts, pains, insults, fears etc. So we take out these buried memories in full awareness of our current actual reality. We re experience the actual past pain, fear just the way we felt when it happened. While at the same time focused on the current reality.

Awareness helps us to put our whole life in context. It makes us aware of our own personal reality especially as it relates to our actual reality. It gives us a 'third party' awareness, an awareness of an outside observer observing one's own self/mind. Not only do we become knowledgeable about our 'outside in' perception patterns and our 'inside out' perception patterns it even gives us the discrepancy between the two. It is this discrepancy that creates all the problems from poverty to restlessness to hunger for more and more and every thing in between.

The goal of awareness is to bring our personal reality (P-R) in line with the real world - the actual reality (A-R). Awareness shows us the gap between the two. In fact the internet is an example full of ways how to fill this gap - by enabling the brain mind relationship to become physically and emotionally super healthy. www.askdryahya.com

** The writer is a professor of social psychology and Sociology.

––––––––––

Sources:

http://knol.google.com/k/knowing-the-difference-between-the-brain-and-mind-through-everyday-life#

http://EzineArticles.com/6543450

http://www.amazon.com/Al-Wai-Wal---Wai-Consciousness-unconsciousness/dp/1453667776/ref=sr_1_1?s=books&ie=UTF8&qid=1316226209&sr=1-1

http://www.amazon.com/Pesonality-Stress-Management-New-Theory/dp/1440459452/ref=sr_1_2?s=books&ie=UTF8&qid=1316226249&sr=1-2

حول مطبوعات الموسوعة العربية الأمريكية
ومنشورات معهد إحياء التراث العربي في المهاجر

Arab American Encyclopedia-USA - Hasan Yahya

About the author

الدكتور حسن عبدالقادر يحيىDr. Hasan A. Yahya

Professor, Dr. Hasan A. Yahya is a Jordania American writer originally born in Palestine. He's the author of American Arab Encyclopedia (AAE), the Honorary Committee Member of the Arab & Muslim Writers Union-(A&MWU), the Dean of the Arab writers in North America, an SME Expert , and president of DryahyaTV. He's an Arab American writer, scholar, poet and retired professor of Sociology. He graduated from Michigan State University with 2 Ph.d degrees. He published 100 books plus (65 Arabic and 35 English & Bilingual), and 500 plus articles on sociology, religion, psychology, politics, poetry, and short stories. Philosophically, his writings concern logic, justice and human rights worldwide. Dr. Yahya is the author of best selling book: Crescentologism: The Moon Theory, and Islam Finds its Way, in English, and 28 Arabic Short Stories in Arabic, all on Amazon, Createspace and Kindle. He's of encyclopedic nature in knowledge, an expert on Race Relations, Arab & Islamic cultures. His main interested in Philosophy, Religion, World affairs and global strategic planning for the purpose of justice and human rights. www.dryahyatv.com From his quotes: "No body is perfect, mentally or physically" and "If people loose their dignity, No one may imagine what they are capable of doing to regain it.

ولد في مجدل يابا من أعمال يافا – فلسطين عام 1944. تلقى علومه الابتدائية في مدرسة بديا الأميرية في الضفة الغربية أيام احتوائها ضمن المملكة الأدردنية الهاشمية وتخرج في جامعة بيروت حاملاً الإجازة في اللغة العربية وآدابها، ودبلوم التأهيل التربوي من كلية القديس يوسف بلبنان، ودبلوم الدراسات العليا (الماجستير) ودكتوراة في الإدارة التربوية من جامعة ولاية ميشيغان بالولايات المتحدة عام 1988، وشهادة الدكتوراه في علم الاجتماع المقارن من الجامعة نفسها عام 1991. عمل في التدريس والصحافة الأدبية. ومنصرف إلى الكتابة في علوم كثيرة تخص علمي النفس والاجتماع والتنمية البشرية ، ألف ونشر العديد من المقالات والكتب باللغتين العربية والإنجليزية ، وله ست مجموعات قصصية وست كتب للأطفال ، وأربع دواوين شعرية باللغتين أيضا. وهو الآن أستاذ متقاعد في جامعة ولاية ميشيغان. وهو عضو جمعية الكتاب العرب والمسلمين في أمريكا الشمالية ومؤسس الموسوعة العربية الأمريكية في الولايات المتحدة ضمن مشروع إحياء التراث العربي في بلاد المهجر .

مؤلفاته:

Arab American Encyclopedia Publications

منشورات الموسوعة العربية الأمريكية

Dr. Hasan Yahya Books - كتب الدكتور: د حسن يحيى

كتب (بالعربية والإنجليزية) ، قام بنشرها الدكتور حسن يحيى ضمن مشروعه: إحياء التراث العربي في المهجر ، بالتعاون مع الموسوعة العربية الأمريكية التي أسسها أيضا لهذا الغرض ومعهد البحوث الإدارية ومطابع شركة البركان وتلفزيون الدكتور يحيى في الولايات المتحدة :

The Arab American Encyclopedia Publications:

In English:

1. Moon Flowers: Poems, Tales & Politics
2. Poetry Diwan: Love, Fears & Hopes
3. Crescentology: A Theory Of Conflict Management And Cultural Normalization
4. Crescentologism: The Moon Theory
5. Brief Arab & Muslim Ethics: For Non-Arabic Speakers (Bilingual)
6. The Beast In Me America: Arabic Folklore, Tales, Stories, & Poetry
7. Personality & Stress Management: A New Theory
8. Arab Palestinian & Jews: Sociological Aproach
9. Legal Adultery: Sexuality & World Cultures
10. Crescentologism: The Moon Theory
11. Islam: Finds Its Way
12. 30 Tales From Faraway Land: Middle Eastern
13. Brief Islamic History (bilingual)
14. Jesus Christ Speaks Arabic
15. فن أدبي جديد Fan Adabi Jadid (bilingual)

16. Protocols of Zion: Trilingual : Spnaish, English & Arabic
17. Prophets Saga: from Adam to Muhammad
18. Al-Akhlaq al-Islamiyyah (Bilingual)
19. Quotes: Love & Humor (Bilingual)
20. Jesus is Different the Prophets History
21. 50 Short Stories (55 words)-Bilingual
22. The Intruder: Bilingual
23. ***Alisha and Other Stories.***
24. 70 Very Short Stories (English)
25. *Short Stories from World Literature (Bilingual)*
26. 65 stories for Children 3-12 , (English)
27. Occupation and Other Stories from World Literature –English
28. 85 Fables & Tales for Children 3 to 12 (English)
29. *Naji al-Ali Art Show.* A Palestinian Artist *Ann Mary Thatcher*
30. Princess Imagination: A New Design Novel (English)
31. Al-Hariri Assemblies (Maqamat al-Hariri (English)
32. Water, Population and Conflict in the Middle East.
33. *Princess Diana Still Alive, A New Novel Design. Ann Mary Thatcher.*
34. *Nietzsche On Christianity*
35. *Bertrand Russell: Roads to Freedom*
36. *The Dangers of the GMS:Slideshow & Presebtation*
37. *Mental Voyage: Ernest HemingwaySuicide Story*
38. *Mental Voyage: Brief Management: Theories & Applications.*
39. *Mental voyage: I Have the Right to be Angry*
40. *Mental Voyage Series: FBI Madness Storm , One Act Play*
41. *Mental Voyage: Nadia: An Innocent Girl from Cairo, Short Story*

42. *Mental Voyage: Brain & Mind Psychology*
43. التعاليم الأخلاقية العربية والإسلامية – باللغتين
44. 28قصة قصيرة بالعربية
45. 55قصة قصيرة للأطفال
46. مناهج البحث العلمي في العلوم الاجتماعية
47. أضواء على الفكر الغربي
48. حالات علاجية لغير القادرين
49. علم الإجتماع التطبيقي
50. حكايات من أمريكا
51. قياسات الذكاء بالعربية
52. نظرية سي القمرية والطبيعة البشرية
53. مقالات في التنميةالإجتماعية
54. ديوان بحر الأماني – شعر
55. ديوان القدر – شعر
56. ديوان لولاك – شعر
57. زوجة السلطان – مجموعة قصصية
58. زوجات للبيع – قصص ومقالات
59. 2000بيت من الشعر العربي
60. الزواج والجنس في العالم
61. كتاب الحب والأبراج
62. قواعد الحب والزواج
63. كبري عقلك : أغاني للكبار.
64. مسرحيات وقصص / الشرط الثالث
65. الإسلام ومصالح البشر
66. أغاني رياض الأطفال – للأطفال
67. الطفلة المثالية – كتاب أطفال
68. حكايات وأغاني للأطفال20/20
69. سلسلة بلادي العربية – أصل الحضارة)للأطفال(
70. 2000بيت من الشعر العربي
71. مضاربات الشعر العربي والمعلقات ـأكثر من 3000 بيت
72. الوعي واللاوعي والسعادة
73. عشر قصص عربية
74. العربية فن : لغير الناطقين بالعربية .
75. محمد) ص(رسول البشرية
76. موجز التاريخ الإسلامي
77. مهارات المعلم وإدارة الفصل – جزء أول
78. مهارات المعلم وإدارة الفصل – جزء ثان

79. اللهم فاشهد – مقالات
80. مقالات في علم النفس
81. عربي في أمريكا – مجموعة قصصية
82. أسس الإدارة ونظرياتها
83. الأسرة العربية في مهب الريح
84. سلسلة التعليم للأطفال باللغتين – 1
85. التعاليم الأخلاقية العربية والإسلامية – باللغتين
86. مسرحية : الدخيل، بالعربية مترجمة عن الإنجليزية
87. مسرحية الدخيل، بالصينية مترجمة عن الإنجليزية
88. مسرحية الدخيل بالإسبانية ، مترجمة عن الإنجليزية
89. فن أدبي جديد خمسون قصة قصيرة جدا : 55 كلمة فقط – باللغتين (bilingual)
90. أفضل القصص :ثلاثون قصة عربية قصيرة
91. قصة عربية قصيرة 70
92. أشعار الربيع العربي : قصائد من العالم العربي
93. قصص عربية قصيرة من الإدب العربي المعاصر .
94. الإحتلال وقصص أخرى – مترجمة من الإدب العالمي
95. سبعون قصة عربية قصيرة جدا.
96. معروف الإسكافي وقصص أخرى من ألف ليلة وليلة
97. قصة التوابع والزوابع لابن شهيد الأندلسي
98. رسالة الغفران لأبي العلاء المعري
99. مقامات بديع الزمان الهمذاني الخمسين بالعربية
100. كتاب كليلة ودمنة لابن المقفع
101. مقامات الحريري الخمسين بالعربية
102. حي بن يقظان لابن طفيل
103. قصص قصيرة من الأدب العربي المعاصر بالعربية
104. الاحتلال وقصص أخرى –مترجمة من الأدب العالمي / 1
105. طبائع الاستبداد للكواكبي
106. باب الإيمان في الصحيحين البخاري ومسلم
107. تفسير الجلالين : سورة البقرة
108. كتاب الطهارة في صحيح مسلم.
109. أشعار الشباب العربي: قصائد من البلاد العربية
110. مقالات أنيس منصور: د. أحمد هيكل 52.
111. خمسون مقالا لأنيس منصور/ 2
112. مقالات لأنيس منصور/ 3 .
113. تفسير سورة الكهف : شريف سيد قطب
114. تفسير سورة الكهف : يوسف القرضاوي

115. الغزال الطائر :قصص ومسرحيات -قادم قريبا

116. صدام حسين : رواية أخرج منها يا ملعون

117. زبيبة والملك: رواية لصدام حسين

118. السأم الباريسي ترجمة أشغار بودلير لمحمد الإحسايني

119. أرض البرتقال الحزين لغسان كنفاني

120. الدفلى: رواية بالعربية لماري رشو

121. الطوفان الأزرق : رواية من الخيال العلمي للكاتب المغربي : أحمد عبدالسلام البقالي

122. في مهب الريح: رواية للكاتب الأردني تيسير دبابنة

أما مقالاته فتزيد على الخمسمائة مقال باللغتين العربية والإنجليزية وهي منشورة على الإنترنت ، وتم جمع بعضها في كتبه الإنجليزية والعربية كل في مجاله .

ويمكن الاتصال به خلال الإيميل الخاص به أو حساب Paypal

drhasanyahya@aol.com